Where to From Here?

A guide for groups working
the Twelve Steps
of RSA

22772 Centre Drive, Suite 205
Lake Forest, CA 92630

COPYRIGHT NOTICE

© 2010 by BlackHawk Canyon Publishers

2 3 4 5 6 7 8 9 10

All rights reserved. No part of this work may be reproduced or transmitted in any form by any means without express, written consent from the publisher.

The author and publisher have taken care in the preparation of this work, but make no expressed or implied warranty of any kind and assume no responsibility for errors or omissions. No liability is assumed for incidental or consequential damages in connection with, or arising out of the use of the information or exercises contained herein.

The characters presented in this work are composite fictions, representing true stories from multiple individuals. The stories have been modified to protect the anonymity of all persons. Any resemblance to any specific person, living or dead, is coincidental.

BlackHawk Canyon Publishers
22772 Centre Dr., Suite 205
Lake Forest, CA 92630

Scripture taken from HOLY BIBLE , NEW INTERNATIONAL VERSION. © Copyright 1973, 1978, 1984 International Bible Society. Used by permission of Zondervan Bible Publishers.

Title: Where to from here? A guide for groups working the twelve steps of RSA.

self-help, psychology, sexual addiction, recovery, religion, spirituality, step study

The Twelve Steps and Twelve Traditions of Alcoholics Anonymous have been reprinted and adapted with the permission of Alcoholics Anonymous World Services, Inc. ("A.A.W.S."). Permission to reprint and adapt the Twelve Steps and Twelve Traditions does not mean that Alcoholics Anonymous is affiliated with this program. A.A. is a program of recovery from alcoholism only – use of A.A.'s Steps and Traditions or an adapted version of its Steps and Traditions in connection with programs and activities which are patterned after A.A., but which address other problems, or use in any other non-A.A. context, does not imply otherwise. Additionally, while A.A. is a spiritual program, A.A. is not a religious program. Thus, A.A. is not affiliated or allied with any sect, denomination, or specific religious belief.

Table of Contents

The Serenity Prayer 4
About Renewed Hope/RSA Ministries 5
The Twelve Steps of RSA 7
The Twelve Traditions of RSA 9
Acknowledgements 10
Introduction 11
Facilitator's Guide 13
Participant's Guide 15
Participation Guidelines 17

Step One 19
Step Two 25
Step Three 33
Step Four 43
Step Five 51
Step Six 57
Step Seven 65
Step Eight 73
Step Nine 83
Step Ten 91
Step Eleven 99
Step Twelve 111

Bibliography 119

The Serenity Prayer

God, grant me the serenity
to accept the things I cannot change;
the courage to change the things I can;
and the wisdom to know the difference.

Living one day at a time;
Enjoying one moment at a time;
Accepting hardships as the pathway to peace;
Taking, as He did, this sinful world
as it is, not as I would have it;
Trusting that He will make all things right
if I surrender to His Will;
That I may be reasonably happy in this life
and supremely happy with Him
Forever in the next.
Amen.

— Reinhold Niebuhr

About Renewed Hope and RSA Ministries

Renewed Hope is a 501 (C) 3, Federally exempt, non-profit corporation whose mission is to produce Christ-centered, 12 step programs and materials for those who struggle with compulsive sexual behaviors and for those who love them. Renewal from Sexual Addiction (RSA) Ministries is our "public face", or the name used for our face-to-face meetings and our online sober recovery community. Currently we have face-to-face meetings in nine states in the U.S. plus a meeting in Canada.

We believe that the cornerstone for our recovery is the power, grace, and love of Jesus Christ. The rest of our recovery "house" is built upon the fellowship of the group, having a safe place to share our struggles, pain, and victories, the accountability of the group, and the mutual support of group members throughout the week.

Our program materials include all of the structure needed to start and run three different types of traditional participation meetings: 1) for men, 2) for women who struggle with sexual addiction, and 3) for spouses of sexually addicted individuals. The addition of the "Where To From Here?" step study guides provides a much needed structure for those desiring more in-depth step work.

The first RSA meeting was held in 1993 and was a men's participation meeting held on the campus of Saddleback Valley Community Church. A group of 24 brave souls walked into the room on that first night and began their journey of sobriety. In 1995 we released our materials for the first Christ-centered program for spouses, and we called it, "Renewal from Co-Sexual Addiction", or "R-CoSA". Committed to working their own program and finding the love they need through their relationship with Christ instead of through their husbands, these courageous women chose to let go of the insanity of attempting to control uncontrollable people, places, and things, and let God control their lives. Later, in 1997, the first RSA meeting for women was started and called, "RSA-W," or Renewal from Sexual Addiction for Women. This meeting is unique in the world as it provides a safe haven for women with compulsive sexual behaviors to gather to share in their strength, hope, and wisdom and seek recovery through their relationship with Christ Jesus. Finally, In 1999 the first RSA Step Study meeting was held, and we began the process of developing the step study guide materials that you hold in your hand today.

If you are not yet a member of RSA, please feel free to join our online sober community at www.rsaministries.org. There you will find a number of resources to help you attain and maintain your recovery. Join us, won't you, and share of your strength and hope in Christ, or borrow some of ours.

The Twelve Steps
Of ROSA

1. We admitted we were powerless over lust – that our lives had become unmanageable.

2. Came to believe that God could restore us to sanity.

3. Made a decision to turn our will and our lives over to the care of God.

4. Made a searching and fearless moral inventory of ourselves.

5. Admitted to God, to ourselves and to another human being the exact nature of our wrongs.

6. Were entirely ready to have God remove all these defects of character.

7. Humbly asked Him to remove our shortcomings.

8. Made a list of all persons we had harmed, and became willing to make amends to them all.

9. Made direct amends to such people wherever possible, except when to do so would injure them or others.

10. Continued to take personal inventory and when we were wrong promptly admitted it.

11. Sought through prayer and meditation to improve our relationship with God praying for knowledge of His will for us, and the power to carry that out.

12. Having had a spiritual awakening as the result of these steps, we tried to carry this message to other lust addicts, and to practice these principles in all our affairs.

The Twelve Traditions of RSA

1. Our common welfare should come first; personal recovery depends upon RSA unity.

2. For our group purpose there is but one ultimate authority — a loving God as He may express Himself in our group conscience. Our leaders are but trusted servants; they do not govern.

3. The only requirement for RSA membership is a desire to stop lusting.

4. Each group should be autonomous except in matters affecting other groups or RSA as a whole.

5. Each group has but one primary purpose—to carry its message to the lustaholic who still suffers.

6. An RSA group ought never endorse, finance or lend the RSA name to any related facility or outside enterprise, lest problems of money, property and prestige divert us from our primary purpose.

7. Every RSA group ought to be fully self-supporting, declining outside contributions.

8. RSA should remain forever nonprofessional, but our service centers may employ special workers.

9. RSA, as such, ought never be organized; but we may create service boards or committees directly responsible to those they serve.

10. RSA has no opinion on outside issues; hence the RSA name ought never be drawn into public controversy.

11. Our public relations policy is based on attraction rather than promotion; we need always maintain personal anonymity at the level of press, radio, internet and films.

12. Anonymity is the spiritual foundation of all our traditions, ever reminding us to place principles before personalities.

Acknowledgements

This work is dedicated to those who came before us, who shared of their experience, hope and wisdom to show us the path of recovery, and to those who have yet to find the path. I would like to express my sincere gratitude to the many people in various recovery rooms and to my patients, all of whom continue to teach me every day.

I give any credit that may come due this work to Our Lord and Savior, Jesus of Nazareth. For it is not of my own wisdom, but His. I have the easy job, I hold the pen, and He dictates.

I thank those who have believed in the importance of this work and who encouraged, guided, and supported me. There is a group of men who have been my friends since high school and now serve as the Board of Directors for Renewed Hope. I would have folded up my little tent and gone home long ago were it not for their continual prodding and oversight: Kenneth Cook, Barn Cochran, Chris Hoffman, and Don Palmer. I also owe an immeasurable debt of gratitude to my mentor, Mal McSwain. I am one of many, many people who owe this humble and wise man the certainty of the knowledge of our salvation. Thanks guys, to all of you, and to your wives and families, for believing in the vision our Lord gave me, and in my ability to steward it well. Also, I thank my good friends David Zailer and Mark Laaser, for their continual support, encouragement, and guidance. Finally, and most importantly, I want to acknowledge the support and encouragement of my best friend and partner in this life, my wife, Shari.

Introduction

Recovering from a life that has been centered on compulsive sexual behaviors is a daunting task for any one. It is a challenge best accepted when you are well prepared and surrounded by supportive people who love you. As a rule, we recommend that step work begin after a person has attained a year of sobriety or more, has a good relationship with a sponsor, and has multiple accountability partners. Due to the nature of step work, it is more likely to threaten one's sobriety than it is to strengthen it.

When many of us arrived at program we were neck-deep in chaos. We had made a complete mess of our lives and had ruined our relationships with families, friends, and others. Some of us had even lost jobs due to our addiction or suffered other financial losses. Some of us had ruined our health. Our lives had become "unmanageable," or as one member put it, "A wrecked train looking for a place to park." We were directed to a place of recovery, where others with similar problems talked about where they had been, what their life was like then, and what it is like now.

We kept coming back, week after week. In time, the chaos that had been our lives began to calm down. We learned to listen to those who had walked this path before us, and we began to find recovery. We found a new relationship with our spirituality, and our sobriety began to grow. However, with all of our history behind us, and so much living yet ahead of us, we found ourselves asking our fellow travelers, "Ok. Where to from here?" That is when we learned about "working the steps." They told us that "step work" is the heart of the program and the tool that God will use to help us attain and maintain sobriety.

As you begin this journey of personal character growth, make sure that you have as much sobriety, support, and spiritual growth as you are able to manage. You will need every bit of it. Through the step work, you will face the people, places and things that lined the road you traveled from where you began, to where you are now. Take your time walking this road. Many of us take as much as a year, or more, to complete the twelve steps. Since you will be working the steps many times in the years ahead, there is no rush to finish. Take heart! The path gets easier, and brighter each time you finish it.

Take the time to open each of your step study sessions with prayer. Ask the Lord to open your eyes to see, and your heart to hear the truths about yourself that He wants you to address. Make sure that as many people as possible know about your endeavors, and are praying for you as well. Also, if you are not able to work the steps in a group format, make sure you maintain regular attendance at your meetings, and keep close and frequent communication with your sponsor and accountability partners. May Our Lord and Savior, Jesus Christ, guide you and comfort you as you walk along this road to recovery.

Blessings,

Laird

Rev., Dr. Laird Bridgman
Founder, Renewed Hope and RSA Ministries

Facilitator's Guide

The following materials are designed to be used in a group setting, led by an individual trained in group facilitation and someone who has already completed his or her own work through the twelve steps. It is beyond the scope of this work to provide such training in detail and these materials are not to be considered sufficient instruction in group facilitation nor as an adequate substitute for such training. When used by a properly trained facilitator, these materials should provide adequate information to help you guide a group of recovering sex addicts through the Twelve Steps of RSA. We offer the few suggestions that follow this paragraph for use by someone with such training and experience.

The number of members in the group is a key factor to a successful group: Too few members and the work goes too quickly and usually lacks depth, too many members and the group goes too slowly and also lacks depth. We have found that the ideal number of members is around 24. However, we've had many groups with over 40 members and some with as few as 6. That goes to show that while the number of participants can play a role, it is not nearly as important as the effort that each member brings to the work.

Most groups will spend an average of 12 – 16 months working through the steps. That means that groups spend an average of one month working through each step. Some steps take a little longer, while others a little less. If a large group is moving slowly, but their work is of good quality, you should consider splitting the group into multiple, smaller groups. At the same time, however, it is important to keep the group moving and to not get bogged down in too much detail or distracted by divisive issues of theology or politics.

We strongly recommend that each individual have his/her own copy of the study guide for groups as well as his/her own copy of the study guide for individuals. The group discussion questions and activities that follow are most useful when all participants have already completed the corresponding individual work in the appropriate section of the "WTFH?" Guide for Individuals, prior to coming to group. If an individual cannot afford to purchase one or both of the books, and if your group cannot arrange to provide a copy to him/her, please contact us directly for assistance (www.rsaministries.org) as we may be able to arrange a scholarship to provide them the needed materials.

The work for each step is divided into three types of activities: 1) Group Discussion Questions (GDQ), 2) Weekly Updates (WU), and 3) Group Activities (GA). A general format for the step study is: 1) opening prayer, participation guideline reading and introductions. Read aloud the step you are working on that week and the introductory materials to each step – 10 minutes, 2) GDQ – 25 minutes, 3) WU – 20 minutes, 4) GA – 20 minutes, and 5) announcements, prayer requests, and closing prayer – 15 minutes. That's a jam-packed 90 minutes!

Each facilitator must decide, based upon the number of participants in each meeting, and the quality of the work being done, how long to allow each member to spend on his or her answer to any given question during each section. The facilitator's role of starting and stopping on time, and that of keeping the group moving and productive within the boundaries established for sharing during group is crucial to a successful group.

Make sure that you have prepared for each group session by reviewing the materials for that week. Also, if there were any discussion questions left over from the previous week, be sure you complete those before moving on.

As a rule, most programs find that it is important to close the meeting to new members by the end of Step Four. This is an outside limit, but the group may be closed earlier. As difficult as it is to turn a hurting person away, the safety of the group is of utmost importance. The work that transpires in the recovery room is highly sensitive. Many of us share things during step work that we have never shared with any other person. It is critical that we are able to count on continuity with our fellow sojourners. We recommend that the members discuss their commitment to the group each week during the first few meetings and agree to commit to making the step work a priority in their lives and being there every week.

We believe it is important to open every meeting in prayer, asking for the Lord's wisdom and guidance as the group seeks His truth in recovery. Some groups have a prayer session prior to each meeting to anoint the room and pray for the work God will be doing in the coming hours.

In terms of structuring the group time itself, we recommend that you have someone from the group read the Participation Guidelines (see page 17) after the opening prayer. Next, have someone else read the current step. Finally, for the fist week, have someone read the introductory comments to the step before beginning the discussion questions or activities. For subsequent weeks when working on the same step, we suggest having someone read a pre-selected portion of the writings from the corresponding sections of the *WTFH? Guide For Individuals* to that step.

However you structure your step study, know that it is a long journey that you will all take together; one of discovery of self and of the Almighty God and His son, Jesus, the Christ.

May your journey be a blessed one.

Laird

Rev., Dr. Laird Bridgman
Founder, Renewed Hope and RSA Ministries

Participant's Guide

The *Where To From Here? Guide for Groups Working the 12 Steps of RSA* is a companion to the *Where to From Here? Guide for Individuals Working the 12 Steps of RSA*. This book is designed for use in group settings to provide structure and direction for working through the 12 steps together. It may be used as a stand-alone work, but it is best suited as a companion to the individual study guide. Most people find they get the most out of the step study experience by working through the individual study guide and then using the Group Discussion Questions for the group meeting.

Before setting out on the step study journey, we recommend that all participants have been working their program actively for a year. Obtaining a year of sobriety is highly desirable prior to starting step study work, as the content of the steps is certain to stir up strong negative emotions. Because a sex addict's best coping skill has always been acting out, it is risky to begin this work until you have developed other coping skills and a strong foundation for your sobriety. On the other hand, others only truly begin to find sobriety after they begin work on the steps, and the work actually improves their sobriety rather than threatening it. Whatever your situation might be with regards to your length of sobriety, seek out the advice of your sponsor, accountability partners, pastor, and/or professional counselor or therapist before you begin.

Two words about participation during a step study group: take risks! The nature of step study work is best exemplified by the saying, "you get out of it what you put into it." Many of us experience anxiety or fear when we have to share in a setting like this. As uncomfortable as it is, it is important to understand that it is as important for us to open our mouths and "let the garbage out" as it is for others to hear and identify with our experience. We all learn from each other's experiences, so do not discount the value of yours to someone else.

A word about procrastination: DON'T! If "progressive internal sobriety" is truly your most important priority, then make time in your schedule to prepare each week, in advance of the meeting. Those who show up unprepared and "wing it" will have sobriety "with wings" that flies away from you when you need it most. Additionally, understand that while your presence at each meeting is crucial to every other member of your group, your "prepared presence" is even more valuable. Make sure you are prepared so that you are giving as much as you are receiving.

Trust in the LORD
with all your heart
and lean not on your own understanding;
in all your ways acknowledge him,
and he will direct your paths.

— Proverbs 3, 5-6

Participation Guidelines

1. There will be no cross talk please. Each person is free to express feelings without interruption. However, the leader has the right to remind the person sharing of guidelines, time limits, etc.

2. We don't give advice. We use the first person, "I," not "we" or "you." If we want to respond to what someone has said, we speak only in terms of our own experience.

3. We speak honestly of where we are today and at this moment. We realize that living in the past or the future is a symptom of our disease and that to heal we must develop a transparent honesty of who we are at each moment.

4. In sharing, rather than displaying our knowledge or insights, we lead with our weaknesses. We work at staying out of our heads and at speaking from our hearts, and take the risk of self-disclosure.

5. We avoid explicit sexual descriptions and sexually abusive language. We also avoid getting sidetracked in issues of theology, semantics, politics, or other divisive issues.

6. If anyone feels uncomfortable with how specific a speaker is being regarding his sexual behaviors then you may indicate so by simply raising your hand. The speaker will then respect your boundaries by being less specific in his descriptions.

7. We work on uncovering and repairing our own defects. We do not recover by focusing on someone else's defects. We avoid self-pity and blaming others.

8. By attending on time and sharing regularly, we give of ourselves to others in the group. We get back recovery.

9. Anonymity and confidentiality are basic requirements. Who and What is shared in the group stays in the group!

10. We work at allowing Christ to transform us through the renewal of our minds. We work at discarding our defensive religious structures and focus on developing our relationship with Christ at a personal level.

Step One

We admitted we were powerless over our lust and that our lives had become unmanageable.

> "There is a principle which is a bar against all information, which is proof against all arguments and which cannot fail to keep a man in everlasting ignorance – that principle is contempt prior to investigation."
>
> — HERBERT SPENCER

There is a moment, for each of us, when we are forced to face the truth about ourselves: That we have allowed our relationship with lust to be the most important thing in our lives. We have become willing to sacrifice everything to maintain our right to choose sin. In that choice, we reject God and put lust on the throne of our life.

Selecting lust as ruler of your life is like electing Hitler to be President. He is not one who rules in your best interests, but in his own. He serves himself, his own ideals, his own morals, and his own rules. He does not care whether others agree with him or even like him. He holds to no authority but his own council. He recognizes no limits or boundaries. As he immediately declares himself monarch for life, and by the time you realize that your life under his rule is not what you thought it would be, you can't get him out of office. He has become too powerful, and has an army of supporters to defend him at any moment. On some days, you forget how bad things are, and even you sing his praises.

When we fully realize that lust is a merciless master, when we understand that we are empty and alone because of lust's rule, and when we finally grasp the idea that we lack the strength to overcome lust on our own, we are finally ready to ask for help and begin recovery.

There was so much chaos going on when we first arrived at this program that we could hardly do the simple things, like show up for our meetings. Fortunately, there were those who had been where we were before us who came along side us and told us over and over to "keep coming back," and to "keep it simple, stupid," and to "lead with the body and the mind will follow." Slowly, as we came to meetings, talked with our sponsors and accountability partners and stayed sober, the air became clearer so that we could breathe again. In the strength of others, and through the grace and love of Jesus, we found "enough" power to begin to win some battles with having lust as the ruler of our life.

Group Discussion Questions

The following questions are to help you define and elaborate on the concepts of powerlessness and unmanageability as they apply to your life. In our step study groups, our willingness to be transparent and share of our experience, strength, and hope is an important contributor to the power of our program. Being nervous about sharing is common to us all. It has been said that courage is not doing something in the absence of fear, but it is doing it anyway, in spite of the fear. Do it afraid. Remember that whatever happens here, whatever is said here, stays here.

1) What is your definition of "powerless"? _____
_____
_____
_____
_____
_____

2) What do you know about your life that leads you to conclude that you have a problem?
_____
_____
_____
_____
_____
_____

3) What was your first sexual experience? How old were you? Were any other people involved, if yes, who and how old were they? _____
_____
_____
_____
_____
_____
_____

4) Describe the progressive nature of your addiction. Make sure you discuss how your life demonstrated tolerance and loss of control. _____
_____
_____
_____
_____
_____

5) Understanding that we pay a "price" for our addictive behaviors, what has your addiction "cost" you? Some examples are relationships, jobs, respect, health and money. Be

as specific as possible. _____
_____
_____
_____
_____

6) When you look over your Addiction History Timeline (see WTFH? For Individuals), did you find any correlation between events in your or your family's life and your addictive behaviors? _____
_____
_____
_____
_____
_____

7) How does creating a family genogram help you understand powerlessness differently?
_____
_____
_____
_____
_____

8) Describe how the word "unmanageable" applies to your life. _____
_____
_____
_____
_____

9) How does admitting that you are powerless over lust and that your life had become unmanageable help you get and stay sober? _____
_____
_____
_____
_____

10) What is the most challenging aspect of Step One for you? _____
_____
_____
_____
_____

Group Activity: Weekly Updates

The Weekly Updates are an important part of the process of developing the new skills that the 12 Steps teach us. Each week, until you have completed this step, make time to check in with each group member on these items:

1. Did you contact your sponsor this week? If yes, how does talking to your sponsor help you? If no, why not? If you do not have a sponsor, what do you need to do to solve that problem? _____
_____
_____
_____
_____
_____

2. Did you make any phone calls to accountability partners and/or group members this week? If yes, how was it helpful? If no, what changes do you need to make for the coming week? _____
_____
_____
_____
_____
_____

3. Did you spend any time in prayer this week? If yes, how was it helpful? If no, what changes do you need to make for the coming week? _____
_____
_____
_____
_____
_____

4. Did you go to Church or attend a Bible study this week? If yes, how was it helpful? If no, what changes do you need to make for the coming week? _____
_____
_____
_____
_____
_____

5. Did you learn anything new about your powerlessness this week? _____
_____
_____
_____

_____
_____
_____
_____

6. Did you learn anything new about the unmanageability of your life? _____
_____
_____
_____
_____
_____
_____

Step Two

Came to believe that God could restore us to sanity.

My sponsor tried again. "David, do you believe in any kind of Higher Power?" I said, "I'm not sure." He said, "Would you be willing to believe in a Higher Power?" I replied, "I'm not sure if I can." He asked, "How do you think all the addicts in your Group are staying sober?" I said, "They have a god, they have a Higher Power." Then he said, "Well, can you go to meetings and believe that the addicts there have a Higher Power that is keeping them sober?" And, I said "Yeah. I can do that." He said, "Then I want you to go to meetings and be around addicts who have a Higher Power. Hang out with them, and start praying to whatever Higher Power that you think is around there that you can come to believe in it." "Okay," I said, "I can do that."

I'm not totally sure when it happened. But over time, I was able to discover many powers that were greater than me. Here's an example. Try to jump up in the air and just stay there. Try it more than once. If you are able to succeed, my hat is off to you. You are a power greater than the power of gravity. I am not.

If you do not believe that electricity is a power greater than you... try putting a light bulb in your hand and make it light up by using your own energy. There is no power in the light bulb.

— David B.

Step Two is often called "The Hope Step," because with this step, there is hope for recovery, and without it there is none. Why is that? In the first step, we learned that we are powerless over our lust and that attempting to manage our lives on our own terms resulted in disaster. What power is there, greater than our own, that would be strong enough to overcome the destructive power of lust? In some recovery rooms, they believe that the power of the group, or just someone other than your self, is sufficient. There is no doubt that there is a power in having a "god," regardless of the power of the god. It seems that humans are designed in such a way as to need a god. Surrendering my own will to the power of the group or someone other than my self was a challenging concept to all of us when we first came to recovery. We learned that if we could not believe in God, that, as a beginning, we could believe in the wisdom of those who had been where we were and had found recovery. They kept telling us that there is a God, who knows us completely and thoroughly, and loves us anyway. And that if we allow Him, He will restore our sanity, and our lives.

Group Discussion Questions

The following 14 questions are topics for discussion. Go over them before you go to Group, and consider your answers well. Be prepared to consider any feedback you may receive. Remember, a group is always stronger than the sum of its individuals. When people sincerely work together for the common Good, all things are possible.

1) How do you know whether God does or does not exist? _____
_____
_____
_____
_____
_____

2) Discuss how your emerging awareness of God has changed so far in your recovery journey. _____
_____
_____
_____
_____
_____

3) What are three ways from general revelation that demonstrate to you that God exists? _____
_____
_____
_____
_____
_____

4) What are three verses that speak to your heart about God? Here are some suggested verses to look up: Psa. 117:2, Matt. 19:26, Acts 26:8, Psa. 139:3, Acts 17:24, Matt. 6:26, 2Cor. 5:18, 1Th. 5:9, James 4:12, Psa. 57:10, Rom. 1:20, Eccl. 3:11, Psa. 19:1. _____
_____
_____
_____
_____
_____

5) If you struggle to believe that God exists, what are your three primary issues? For some of us, we have to start with "being willing to become willing" to believe. Are you willing to start there and ask God to reveal Himself to you, if He exists? Ask the group if someone is willing to assist you in "knowing how to know" how God reveals Himself.

6) Discuss how your view of your earthly father has clouded your concept of your heavenly father. _____

7) Describe the miracles performed by Jesus from these verses: Matt 8: 1-4, Mark 4:35-41, Luke 5:17-26, Matt 9:27-31, and Luke 7:11-17. _____

8) Discuss how reading about these miracles impacts you. How do they change your beliefs about Jesus, God, and yourself? Do you believe these are actual historical events? Do you believe God still performs miracles? _____

9) Do you believe that God can restore your sanity? Discuss why or why not. _____

10) Do you believe He wants to? Are you willing to allow Him to do so? _____

11) Do you believe it is possible for you to change? Discuss. _____

_____
_____
_____
_____

12) Who do you know, or whom have you heard of, who has a significant amount of recovery? Describe the quality and quantity of their recovery as best as you understand it. _____
_____
_____
_____
_____

13) How does their recovery impact your belief in your own ability to recover? _____
_____
_____
_____
_____
_____

14) If you do not know anyone whose recovery inspires hope for yourself, discuss what does inspire you to hope for recovery for yourself. _____
_____
_____
_____
_____

Weekly Updates

The Weekly Updates are an important part of the process of developing the new skills that the 12 Steps teach us. Each week, until you have completed this step, make time to check in with each group member on these items:

1. Did you contact your sponsor this week? If yes, how does talking to your sponsor help you? If no, why not? If you do not have a sponsor, what do you need to do to solve that problem? _____

_____
_____
_____
_____
_____
_____

2. Did you make any phone calls to accountability partners and/or group members this week? If yes, how was it helpful? If no, what changes do you need to make for the coming week? _____

_____
_____
_____
_____
_____
_____

3. Did you spend any time in prayer this week? If yes, how was it helpful? If no, what changes do you need to make for the coming week? _____

_____
_____
_____
_____
_____
_____

4. Did you go to Church or attend a Bible study this week? If yes, how was it helpful? If no, what changes do you need to make for the coming week? _____

_____
_____
_____
_____
_____

Group Activity

For this coming week, will you all commit to praying a short prayer, such as The Serenity Prayer or the Prayer of St. Ambrose, once each day? Just a short invocation in the morning (or whenever you start your day) is all that is required. It certainly won't hurt anything. Next meeting, you will share with the group how this activity impacted you.

For those who have difficulty connecting with God, we recommend the Prayer of St. Ambrose, of Milan. It has been effective in helping many people connect with the Holy Spirit. For those who have not had that trouble, we recommend the modified version of the Serenity Prayer. In this exercise, we will be applying the "K.I.S.S." principle (Keep It Simple, Stupid). Since we are addicts, it is all too easy for us to make things harder than they need to be, and which inevitably results in failure for us. Therefore, we will reduce our spirituality to as simple an exercise as it can be.

1. Find a quiet comfortable place where you feel safe and will not be disturbed.

2. Take a few deep breaths to relax your body.

3. Try to clear your mind by focusing your attention on the inside of your closed eyelids. It's the one place where you can see something while looking at nothing! Do this for about 20 seconds.

4. Pray either the St. Ambrose prayer or the Serenity Prayer. Spend about 2 or 3 minutes on quiet meditation on the prayer:

a. Prayer of St. Ambrose:

"Oh Lord, teach me to seek you, and reveal yourself to me when I seek you. For I cannot seek you unless your first teach me, nor find you unless you first reveal yourself to me. Let me seek you in longing, and long for you in seeking. Let me find you in love, and love you in finding. Amen."

b. Serenity Prayer:

"God, grant me the serenity to accept the things I cannot change, the courage to change the things I can, and the wisdom to know the difference. Help me to live one day at a time, to enjoy one moment at a time, and to accept hardships as the pathway to peace. Lord, help me, as you did, to accept this sinful world as it is, not as I would have it. I will trust that You will make all things right if I surrender to Your Will; That I may be reasonably happy in this life and supremely happy with You forever in the next. Amen"

5. Read the prayer in short sections so that you can repeat it with your eyes closed. Over the next few days, you will be able to say the entire prayer from memory.

6. Allow the prayer to fill your mind. Be aware of distracting thoughts, notice them and then return to the prayer. Be mindful of any emotions that arise. Watch them like a leaf on a stream and allow them to pass. Then return to the prayer.

7. Now spend a few minutes listening for the voice of God. The Holy Spirit may touch your heart, or your mind. Be open to these new experiences, and share them with your group.

8. Each week for the next eight weeks, check in with each other on how the daily meditation and prayer is impacting you. Does the daily prayer:

1. Help you to believe in God in a new way? _____
_____
_____
_____
_____
_____

2. Impact you positively in other ways? How? _____
_____
_____
_____
_____
_____

Step Three

We made a decision to turn our wills and our lives over to the care of God.

> "Everyone who calls on the name of the Lord will be saved."
>
> — *Romans 10:13*

Step Three challenges us to surrender control of our lives to God. When we first heard this challenge we wondered how this works: How does one actually turns one's life over to an invisible, all-powerful being? What's more, we weren't sure why He would want our lives anyway...being fairly messed up and useless as they were. God was certainly not getting any bargains on this deal. None the less, we were quite certain that we were unable to do anything further but create more chaos, so we did our best to give Gold control: We had reached our "bottom," and became willing to learn how to apply the word "surrender" to our lives.

Many of us made a decision to recommit our life to Him. Still others of us worked at wanting to learn how to believe. Yet, for every person who worked this simple program, many of us made a decision for Christ for the first time in our lives. Others grew in our spiritual life and daily walk with God. In our life before recovery, we believed we were God and lived our lives as if we were omniscient and omnipotent. Many have described the development of spirituality in recovery in this way: First, "we came" - as in we came to these rooms of recovery; the "we came to" - as in we woke up from a bad dream, and then "we came to believe" - in a God who could restore us to sanity, who loved us and wanted to be involved in our lives. In Step Three we learn how to understand the nature of temptation and the power of Jesus Christ to overcome Satan's lies by renewing our minds. Most importantly, we learn how to turn our lives over to the care of God.

Our mentors and sponsors tell us that recovery is a process, not a destination. In Step Three we make "a decision" that results in our setting off upon this journey of spiritual growth. We can only start where we are, not where we aren't. We begin Step Three by identifying where we are in our spirituality, and then we identify the blocks to our growth and our ability to take the next tiny step forward. We have to look at our ideas of what faith is, and where we stand on the matter; we have to consider whether surrender is a concept we can personally embrace; we have to learn the fullness of what repentance really is; and we have to build the skill of discipline in order to nurture our own spiritual growth. This process of spiritual growth is one of progress, not perfection. At times, it seems as exciting as watching paint dry, and at other times it is the most powerful, wonderul and life-changing event in our lives.

Group Discussion Questions

The first step in turning our lives over to God is to decide who it is we are going to turn our lives over to.

1. Who did Jesus claim to be? Read the following verses and discuss His claims: John 5:24, 6:35, 6:51, 10:9, 10:11, and 11:25. _____
_____
_____
_____

2. Who was Jesus of Nazareth? Others claim that Jesus was just a "good teacher." Discuss how this claim is valid and not valid. _____
_____
_____
_____

3. Others claim that Jesus was a lunatic, a crazy man, who claimed to be God but was not. Discuss the pros and a cons of this perspective. _____
_____
_____
_____
_____

4. Still others claim that Jesus was a liar. In other words, that he was a charlatan; he purposely deceived people about his identity to gain power and control over others. Discuss the pros and cons of this perspective. _____
_____
_____
_____
_____

5. Finally, others believe that Jesus was exactly who He said he was, the Messiah. Discuss whether or not you believe Jesus was the Christ and why. _____
_____
_____
_____
_____

Putting Jesus on the Throne of Your Life

The second step is to make a decision to surrender our life to His control. If you have never made a decision to accept Jesus as your personal savior, then this is a good first step. For others, this is a good time to recommit your life to Jesus. And for those of you not ready to take the step of establishing a personal relationship with a personal savior, we encourage you to work with your best understanding of God the Father, and find someone who can assist you in addressing whatever is in the way for you to commit your life to Jesus. When you are ready, you can establish a relationship with God by simply, and sincerely reciting this simple prayer:

"God, I know that I am a sinner. I know that I deserve the consequences of my sin. I humbly prostrate myself before you now, Lord, to ask for forgiveness, trusting in Jesus Christ as my Savior. I believe that His death and resurrection provided for my forgiveness. I trust in Jesus, and Jesus alone as my personal Lord and Savior. In the name of the Father, the Son, and the Holy Spirit! Amen!"

For those of us who have been down the path of recommitment many times in the past, this may bring up some particular resentment and/or issues about what you think God should have done for you in the past. You know…we committed our life to God and swore "never again, Lord," only to fall into temptation's trap again a short time later. You will have the opportunity to deal with your resentments with God in Step 4, but for now, every journey, no matter how long it is, begins with a single step; getting right with God is another step along your path. You can't go further down the path by skipping this step. This step is not really about "swearing off" from ever acting out again, it is about cleaning house, spiritually, so that I can walk free of the burdens of my past.

If you want to, make a decision for Christ for the first time (or if you just did), or to recommit your life to Christ anew, see your group facilitator for assistance. Some groups prefer to meet these needs as part of the regular meeting time, and some prefer to do so outside the meeting time and with the assistance of pastoral staff.

Group Activity #1

The act of turning one's life over to the care of God is a conscious decision to surrender "my will" to "His will." We have found that making this decision a part of the group process to be a helpful event. Some groups prefer to do it simply and corporately, while others prefer a more semi-private ceremony. Here is a suggestion for your consideration:

Have each person in the group read the following statement aloud:

"I (name) acknowledge that I have led my life, to this point in time, more according to my plan than God's plan. Beginning with this moment, I choose to become more skilled at living each day at a time, each moment at a time, and to seek His will and direction for each moment of my life. I ask for the group's help and support in accomplishing that goal, and I pledge my availability to everyone in this group."

We recommend that each member of the group read this individually. Depending upon the size of the group, this may take some time, but we have found that it is well worth it.

Weekly Updates

The Weekly Updates are an important part of the process of developing the new skills that the 12 Steps teach us. Each week, until you have completed this step, make time to check in with each group member on these items:

1. Did you contact your sponsor this week? If yes, how does talking to your sponsor help you? If no, why not? If you do not have a sponsor, what do you need to do to solve that problem? _____
_____
_____
_____
_____
_____

2. Did you make any phone calls to accountability partners and/or group members this week? If yes, how was it helpful? If no, what changes do you need to make for the coming week? _____
_____
_____
_____
_____
_____

3. Did you spend any time in prayer this week? If yes, how was it helpful? If no, what changes do you need to make for the coming week? _____
_____
_____
_____
_____
_____

4. Did you go to Church or attend a Bible study this week? If yes, how was it helpful? If no, what changes do you need to make for the coming week? _____
_____
_____
_____
_____
_____

Also, check in with everyone on the impact of their continued daily prayer. Continue this activity for at least 8 weeks.

5. Allow each person to comment on how saying The Serenity Prayer or The Prayer of St. Ambrose changed him or her. _____
_____
_____
_____
_____

6. Does talking to God (prayer) change your awareness of Him in any way? If so, how?
_____
_____
_____
_____
_____

7. Has a daily prayer impacted you positively in any other ways? How? _____
_____
_____
_____

Group Activity #2
Satan's Lies/God's Truths

One of the most important changes to make in recovery is to learn to identify our own "permissive beliefs," which are the mechanisms in our minds that allow us to act out; and to change them into appropriate, Christ-like beliefs. We fondly refer to this exercise as "Satan's Lies and God's Truth." For this exercise have someone volunteer to be the group "recorder." The group members are to identify and express as many permissive beliefs as they can think of and the recorder writes them all down. This exercise works best if the group has access to a chalk board, white board, or a flip chart, but even an old fashioned legal pad will work just fine. Then, the group will take each of Satan's lies and challenge it with God's truth. The idea is to end up with a better, more helpful and Christ-like belief at the end. The recorder records all of these as well. Some groups like to make copies of this exercise and make it available to all members. Here is a sample:

Satan's Lie	**God's Truth**	**Verse**
No one will know.	I know, God knows, Often my spouse knows!	1 Cor 4:5

This exercise can take several weeks to complete, but do not be in a rush. Be thorough, and be patient.

1. Brainstorm as many permissive beliefs (No one will know, I deserve it, It won't hurt anyone, etc...) as the group can come up with. _____

_____
_____
_____
_____
_____
_____
_____
_____

2. Create a "lie busting" counter belief, God's Truth, for each permissive belief. _____

_____
_____
_____
_____
_____
_____
_____
_____

3. Identify a verse to accompany each of the new beliefs. _____
_____
_____
_____
_____

4. Make a copy of the list and hand out to each member. _____
_____
_____
_____
_____

Individual Activity: A Daily Walk

Turning our life over to the care of God is not like a birthday – something we celebrate one day out of every 365. Those who have preceded us in recovery have shared with us the wisdom of practicing a daily "walk" with God. "What, exactly, am I supposed to do?" we asked them. They shared several key principles with us:

1) Start every day with a few minutes of reading in the Bible.

2) Spend a few minutes in prayer. Our sister ministry, Operation Integrity, uses a daily prayer in their recovery work. This week, instead of the prayer of St. Ambrose or the Serenity Prayer, we recommend substituting the O.I. prayer:

    i. *"Lord Jesus, I pray that I will learn to desire obedience more than blessing or comfort, and to know that the greatest blessing in life is to live obedient to Your will. May I learn to better give up my will and find my complete and total satisfaction in Your will. My self-centeredness destroys me, but seeking you and doing your will brings life to me. Realizing this, I have decided that my mind, my heart, and my will, will be directed to You. I will find my purpose and identity in knowing you more personally & living more powerfully according to your Spirit. Amen"**

    ii. As before, spend 2 to 3 minutes saying this prayer.

3) Talk with Jesus throughout the day, not just when you formally pray.

4) Participate in a Bible study on a regular basis.

5) Find a body of believers with whom you can fellowship and worship every week.

6) Keep a prayer journal.

7) Ask your accountability partners to help you stay accountable to these disciplines.

8) Share the impact of these activities upon you with your group.

*Copyright 2007 Operation Integrity. Reprinted with permission.

Step Four

We made a searching and fearless moral inventory of ourselves.

> "Any life, no matter how long and complex it may be, is made up of a single moment — the moment in which a man finds out, once and for all, who he is."
>
> — Jorge Luis Borges

There is much more to life than being physically sober. There is much more to sobriety than having our obsession for lust removed. Our addiction left us broken and bleeding, empty and alone. Recovery in Christ offers us the fullness of life. In fact, Jesus said that He came to offer us forgiveness so that we could be full of His joy and that our joy would be complete.

> "I have told you this so that my joy may be in you and that your joy may be complete".
>
> — John 15:11

The ability to have joy, however, requires us to have emotional maturity. There is an old saying in program, "There is good news and bad news about recovery: The good news is that you get your feelings back. The bad news is you get your feelings back!" We have learned that emotions are an all or nothing, package deal. We can't pick just the positive emotions and skip past the negative ones. In order to be able to experience the positive ones we must also be able to experience the negative ones. The Fourth Step is the beginning of our work at developing emotional maturity.

Emotional Maturity

> "Just WHAT IS emotional maturity? One author defines it this way: development from a state of taking to a state of giving and sharing. There's also a spiritual principle involved - development from natural impulses and responses of human nature to the principle of loving one's neighbor as himself or herself."
>
> — Herbert W. Armstrong

Of all of the steps, this one is the most arduous to some of us. It requires us to look with sober eyes at our character defects and to do so with painstaking attention to detail. It would be so much easier to just gloss right over these issues and say to ourselves, "OK, I messed up. Next topic!" However, if we are to grow, we must look at not only the fact of our defects, but also at the mechanisms which give them life and longevity. This work is almost impossible to do solely in the context of a group setting. We must be willing to take the time to work through all the detail on our own and then to share what we have learned with the group.

In order to recover, we must learn to be aware of our weaknesses so that we can address them. You can't fix something if you don't know what's broken. When we share with the group it helps us to gain new perspectives, and to say it aloud helps to make it real. Additionally, our sharing is one way we give back to the group, as we never know when someone will identify something of their own experience in ours, and be helped move another step down their own path of recovery. Sometimes it is easier to see it in others first, before you can learn to see it in yourself.

Our ability to be honest with ourselves about our character defects may be limited by our own fears and resentments. Are we afraid of facing the truth of who we are? Many of us attempted to avoid this step for fear of telling someone else what is on the list. The good news is that in The Fourth Step we only have to write this stuff down and look at it ourselves.

My Mind Is My Garden,
My Thoughts Are My Seeds.
I Will Harvest Either Flowers or Weeds.

— *Anonymous*

Group Discussion Questions

The following group discussion questions will be helpful only to the degree that each group member has successfully completed his or her own fears and resentment work (see WTFH? Guide for Individuals).

1) What were your top three resentments? _____
_____
_____
_____
_____
_____

2) How were your resentments impacting you and in what areas (S.E., S.R., A., etc…)? _
_____
_____
_____
_____
_____

3) Discuss the "new view" that you developed to address those resentments. _____
_____
_____
_____
_____
_____

4) What were your top three fears? _____
_____
_____
_____
_____
_____

5) Describe your new view for how to think about each of those situations so that you were no longer afraid, but able to trust God. _____
_____
_____
_____
_____
_____

6) Discuss how reviewing your sexual behavior list helped you in your perspectives on yourself and your sexuality. _____
_____
_____
_____
_____
_____

7) Discuss how completing your repentance work (as described in the *WTFH? Guide For Individuals*) has impacted you. _____
_____
_____
_____
_____
_____

8) In the *WTFH? Guide for Individuals,* you completed a personal moral inventory, share the grades you gave yourself with the group. Comment on areas of strength and weakness, and how you will work on the areas of weakness. _____
_____
_____
_____
_____
_____

Mastering Yourself

*"Knowing others is intelligence; knowing yourself is true wisdom.
Mastering others is strength; mastering yourself is true power.
If you realize that you have enough, you are truly rich."*

— *Tao Te Ching*

Group Activity: Coping Cards

This activity requires a stack of 3 X 5 index cards, approximately 3 to 5 cards for each member. Give each member 3 or 4 index cards, a pen or pencil, and the list of "Satan's Lies and God's Truths" from the your Step 3 work. Explain the coping card as follows and have each member write out at least three coping cards and share them with the group before the end of group.

The "coping card" is an excellent tool for dealing with temptation.

1. On the front of the card, write one of the permissive beliefs across the top.
2. Beneath that, write the opposing God's Truth belief.
3. On the back, write down three alternate activities (other than acting out),
4. and write out the corresponding Scripture verse.

Here is an example.

Front:

Satan's Lie

No one will know.

God's Truth

I know.
God knows.
My spouse will know (if he/she doesn't already).

Back:

Scripture

I Corinthhians 4:5

"Therefore judge nothing before the appointed time; wait till the Lord comes. He will bring to light what is hidden in darkness and will expose the motives of men's hearts. At that time each will receive his praise from God."

Healthy Activities

1. Call sponsor or accountability partners
2. Go for a walk or exerciese.
3. Go to a meeting.
4. Have coffee with a friend.

These cards should be kept on your person, so that they are available when needed. Keep them in a back pocket, or a purse or briefcase. Just make sure you have access to them when you least think you'd need them!

Weekly Updates

The Weekly Updates are an important part of the process of developing the new skills that the 12 Steps teach us. Each week, make time to check in with each group member on these items:

1) Check in with everyone on the impact of his or her continued daily prayer. Continue this activity for at least 8 weeks.

a) Allow each person to comment on how saying The Serenity Prayer or The Prayer of St. Ambrose changed him or her.

b) Does talking to God (prayer) change your awareness of Him in any way? How?
_____
_____
_____
_____
_____

c) Has a daily prayer impacted you positively in any other ways? How?
_____
_____
_____
_____
_____

2) Did you make any new coping cards during the past week? If yes, describe them.
_____
_____
_____
_____
_____

3) Did you use the coping cards during this past week? If yes, were they helpful? If they were not helpful, how can you modify them to make them so? If you did not use them, why not? _____
_____
_____
_____
_____

Step Five

Admitted to God, to ourselves, and to another human being the exact nature of our wrongs.

> "Josh Billings said, "It is not only the most difficult thing to know oneself, but the most inconvenient one, too." Human beings have always employed an enormous variety of clever devices for running away from themselves, and the modern world is particularly rich in such stratagems"
>
> — John W. Gardner

Step Five is about embarrassment, courage and shame, although not necessarily in that order. Shame is a painful emotion that we experience when we are aware that we have done something improper, dishonorable, or ridiculous. Step Four required us to list every dishonorable, improper and ridiculous thing we've ever done. Now we have to share all of that shame-inducing history with someone else.

Confession

> "If we confess our sins, He is faithful and just and will forgive us our sins, and purify us from all unrighteousness."
>
> — 1 John 1:9

Shame, on the one hand, is an emotion we can experience all by ourselves or with a huge crowd; embarrassment, on the other hand, is an emotion we only experience in the presence (real or imagined) of another. While Step Four was a very effective shame-producing machine, Step Five's products are embarrassment and courage. "Courage?" we asked. "Yes," we were told, "enough courage to complete Step Five in spite of the overwhelming shame and embarrassment." We are not simply making a list of our shortcomings for God: He is already aware of these. However, by having a conversation with our personal Higher Power, the things we need to change are revealed to us. Think of it as a sort of 'Confession'. The reason for Confession is to give all these things to God, and get them out of your life, so they will not come back to haunt your soul later. It is important to tell another human being as well, because once our wrongs are out in the open, there is no longer any reason to feel shame over them, and we can continue the healing process. Many times, another person's input can be the difference between success and failure. It is a difficult but necessary step in recovery. Confession really is good for the soul.

The other key concept in Step Five is that we have to confess the "exact" nature of our wrongs...we cannot soft-pedal it to ourselves or to others. We must be at least "rigorously honest", if not even "brutally honest" in how we examine and portray our wrongs.

Group Discussion Questions

1) Are you willing to tell someone ALL of your secrets? Is there something from your past that you are still considering taking to your grave in silence? _____
_____
_____
_____
_____
_____

2) What are your fears about dong the Fifth Step? _____
_____
_____
_____
_____
_____

3) Why can it be more difficult for you to admit your wrongs to another human being than it is to yourselves or to your Higher Power? _____
_____
_____
_____
_____
_____

4) If you aren't yet willing to do your Fifth Step, where can you find this willingness? ___
_____
_____
_____
_____
_____

5) What fears, excuses, or distractions do you have to doing your Fifth Step? _____
_____
_____
_____
_____
_____

6) Step Five requires us to confess our sins to God and to another human being. Do you have any obstacles to confessing to God or to another human? If so, list them here: ___
_____

7) What actions will you need to take to overcome any of the above obstacles? _____

8) List the person(s) with whom you are considering sharing your Fifth Step: _____

9) Discuss what you know about this person(s) with the group and why you think this person(s) is a good choice with whom to share your Fifth Step. _____

10) What are the disadvantages of sharing with this person? _____

11) Detail the specific date, time and location of your meeting with this person(s), and share with the information with the group and ask for prayer coverage during that time._

12) Schedule an "after Fifth Step" contact with several accountability partners for support and debriefing afterwards. Detail those contacts and arrangements here: _____

_____
_____
_____
_____
_____

Weekly Updates

The Weekly Updates are an important part of the process of developing the new skills that the 12 Steps teach us. Each week, until you have completed this step, make time to check in with each group member on these items:

1. Did you contact your sponsor this week? If yes, how does talking to your sponsor help you? If no, why not? If you do not have a sponsor, what do you need to do to solve that problem? _____
_____
_____
_____
_____

2. Did you make any phone calls to accountability partners and/or group members this week? If yes, how was it helpful? If no, what changes do you need to make for the coming week? _____
_____
_____
_____
_____
_____

3. Did you spend any time in prayer this week? If yes, how was it helpful? If no, what changes do you need to make for the coming week? _____
_____
_____
_____
_____
_____

4. Did you go to Church or attend a Bible study this week? If yes, how was it helpful? If no, what changes do you need to make for the coming week? _____
_____
_____
_____
_____

5. Check in with everyone on the impact of his or her continued daily prayer. Continue this activity for at least 8 weeks.

a. Allow each person to comment on how saying The Serenity Prayer or The Prayer of St. Ambrose changed him or her. _____
_____
_____
_____

b. Does talking to God (prayer) change your awareness of Him in any way? If so, how?
_____
_____
_____

c. Has a daily prayer impacted you positively in any other ways? How?
_____
_____
_____

6. Did you make any new coping cards during the past week? If yes, describe them.
_____
_____
_____
_____
_____

7. Did you use the coping cards during this past week? If yes, were they helpful? If they were not helpful, how can you modify them to make them so? If you did not use them, why not? _____
_____
_____
_____
_____
_____

Step Six

We were entirely ready to have God remove all these defects of character.

> "Submit to God and be at peace with him; in this way prosperity will come to you."
>
> — Job 22:21

What does it mean to "be entirely ready"? It means to be completely prepared, spiritually, emotionally, and psychologically. Our step work thus far has helped to prepare us emotionally and psychologically, to let God remove our character defects. We have dealt with our denial, looked honestly at our behaviors and history, and faced our shame and embarrassment.

> "Here a great number of disabled people used to lie—the blind, the lame, the paralyzed. One who was there had been an invalid for thirty-eight years. When Jesus saw him lying there and learned that he had been in this condition for a long time, he asked him, 'Do you want to get well?'"
>
> — John 5: 3-6

It's one thing to recognize our shortcomings – it's quite another to experience their removal. In recovery, for all of us, change is necessary, and we have to learn how to process information differently. When we surrender our defects of character, we experience ourselves, others, and our world, entirely differently. For example, we can no longer rely on our grandiose notions that we are always right and the problem lies with everyone else. Instead, we have to walk in humility, facing the reality of our mistakes and limitations every day, acknowledging when we are the problem and working to restore peace with our fellow man.

Giving up control, and thus being and feeling quite vulnerable, is very hard for us. This vulnerability is essential, however, if we are to allow His healing to mature in us. Even as we allow God to remove our shortcomings, we still have urges to control how He does it. God cannot work that way. As we learn to "let go and let God," He will reshape us according to His master design for our personhood and our lives. Humility is the fruit born of accepting the fact that God is the creator of all and that we are not. We must trust that He will restore us to be who and what were designed to be.

> "Then Jesus said to him, 'Get up! Pick up your mat and walk.' At once the man was cured; he picked up his mat and walked."
>
> — John 5: 8-9

Group Discussion Questions

> *"Therefore, since we are surrounded by such a great cloud of witnesses, let us strip off everything that hinders and the sin that so easily entangles, and let us run with perseverance the race marked out for us."*
>
> — *Hebrews 12:1*

In Step Six we must continue our preparation by cleaning our house spiritually with repentance. (See the *WTFH? Guide For Individuals* for guidelines on the mechanics of how repentance works.) The following discussion questions will help the group process the concept of character defects and how we learn to allow God to remove them.

1) What are "character defects?" _____
_____
_____
_____
_____
_____
_____

2) What are the most damaging defects in your character? _____
_____
_____
_____
_____
_____
_____

3) What are the biggest defects in your character that you have never shared with someone else? _____
_____
_____
_____
_____
_____
_____

4) This may sound like a silly question, but why do we have to have our character defects removed? Why can't we keep our "warts?" _____
_____
_____
_____
_____
_____
_____

5) Can the leopard really change his spots? Can people really change? If yes, give some examples of people you know who have changed character defects.
_____
_____
_____
_____
_____

6) Have you ever allowed God to remove a defect of character? What was it like having it "removed?" Was it painful? Is it completely gone and never returned?
_____
_____
_____
_____
_____

7) What methods does God use to remove character defects? _____
_____
_____
_____
_____
_____

8) Do you believe God can and will remove your defects of character? If no, why not? _
_____
_____
_____
_____
_____

9) What action steps do you need to take to prepare yourself to allow God to remove your character defects? _____
_____
_____
_____
_____
_____

10) What emotions do you feel when you think about having all of your character defects removed? _____
_____

11) What do you imagine your life will be like once all of your character defects are gone? _____

The following questions are for group discussion AFTER the individual Step Six work has been completed.

12) What does it mean to be "entirely ready" for God to remove your defects of character? Are you "entirely ready?" If not, what is in the way for you?
_____

13) What defects do you have that you really don't want to let go of? _____

14) What defects do you have that you believe cannot be removed and why?
_____

15) What defects have you attempted to remove on your own and how well did you succeed? _____

16) What defects have you already been able to allow God to begin work on? Describe how you "became entirely ready," the "event" of your surrendering your defect, and what the daily process is like?

17) Sometimes, God removes character defects in a single stroke. Do you have any defects that God has already removed completely? Describe what happened and what its like now.

Weekly Updates

The Weekly Updates are an important part of the process of developing the new skills that the 12 Steps teach us. Each week, until you have completed this step, make time to check in with each group member on these items:

1) Did you contact your sponsor this week? If yes, how does talking to your sponsor help you? If no, why not? If you do not have a sponsor, what do you need to do to solve that problem? _____
_____
_____
_____
_____

2) Did you make any phone calls to accountability partners and/or group members this week? If yes, how was it helpful? If no, what changes do you need to make for the coming week? _____
_____
_____
_____
_____
_____

3) Did you spend any time in prayer this week? If yes, how was it helpful? If no, what changes do you need to make for the coming week? _____
_____
_____
_____
_____
_____

4) Did you go to Church or attend a Bible Study this week? If yes, how was it helpful? If no, what changes do you need to make for the coming week?_____
_____
_____
_____
_____
_____

5) How has your prayer life changed since you started working the steps? _____
_____

6) Have your experience of God changed during this time? If yes how? _____

7) Did you make any new coping cards during the past week? If yes, describe them.

8) Did you use the coping cards during this past week? If yes, were they helpful? If they were not helpful, how can you modify them to make them so? If you did not use them, why not? _____

Group Activity

For the coming week, select one character defect that you are ready to allow God to remove. Ask two other members of the group to serve as accountability partners for you in your continued work at allowing God to remove your character defects. Take a few minutes to describe to the group what defect you are willing to have God remove.

a) The defect I am going to work to allow God to remove is: _____
_____
_____
_____

b) My two accountability partners are:

(1) _____
    (a) Phone: _____
    (b) Email: _____

(2) _____
    (a) Phone: _____
    (b) Email: _____

Step Seven

Humbly asked Him to remove our shortcomings.

"Know that the love of thyself doth hurt thee more than anything else in the world. On this defect, that a man inordinately loves himself, hangs almost all in thee that thou hast to root out and overcome; and, when this evil has been once conquered and brought under, soon will there be great peace and tranquility…'Son,' says Christ to us, 'leave thyself, and thou shalt find Me.'"

— De Imitatione Christi

Thomas a' Kempis (1379-1471)

English translation by Rev. Dr. Joel C. Brothers, ND, SHD

Step 6 helped us to prepare ourselves for the work of letting God remove our character defects. First, we had to learn how to be humble. Some have defined humility as a willingness to choose God's will over our own. Others have defined it as an ability to see our weaknesses along with our strengths and thus realize that we are no better than our fellow man. Additionally, we have learned a general principle of addict behaviors: we tend to hang on to what we have, no matter how bad it is, until we get something better to replace it.

Humble yourselves before the Lord, and He will lift you up.

— James 4:10

In Step 7, we will practice specific spiritual principles in our daily affairs, instead of continuing to utilize our character defects. When we ask God to remove our shortcomings we must tackle each defect specifically. We have found that a very broadbrush prayer, like "Lord, please remove all my shortcomings" has little effect - sort of like praying for world peace. However, when we pray specifically, "Lord I turn my shortcoming of pride over to you today. Please replace it with your grace and humility." we find that one day at a time, one moment at a time, we become less and less prideful, and more and more humble.

Step 7 helps us to engage in a process of spiritual growth where we watch God turn our character defects into character assets: Impatience will be replaced with patience, pride will be converted into humility, and self-centeredness will turn into a servant's heart. Our effort is to become more like Christ, each and every day.

May Our Lord grant each of you an extra measure of patience as you begin this work.

A Prayer About Being More Humble Before God

"Most precious lord Jesus, gentle and wonderful God, I love you. I confess to you that I want my way. I want what I want the way I want it. Too often when I pray, I pray to get you to give me what I want. My high-sounding phrases, my "Amens", my "Praise Gods", too often are not what is really in me. Too often I come to you, O Lord, hoping you will deliver for me what I want rather than what you want for me. I am sorry. I am so sorry about trying to push what I want onto you and praying for you to deliver to me what I want. Please forgive me. Forgive me for being selfish and thinking only of myself. Forgive me for being so ego-filled and not thinking about you instead of thinking about what you want for me and from me. Help me to be more humble in your sight. Help me to want only your will for my life. I give you praise this day for standing by me even when I turn selfish. I give you praise for not deserting me even when I desert your will for my life. Please help me to do better than I have done. All these things I humbly pray in the name of my most Blessed Lord Jesus Christ. Amen."

The above prayer is a suggestion to demonstrate how you can practice humility before God. However, you may prefer to write your own prayer, or modify the one above in your own style. Use the space below to do your "word-smithing."

Group Discussion Questions

1) What is humility? _____
_____
_____
_____
_____
_____
_____

2) How is self-reliance related to humility? _____
_____
_____
_____
_____
_____
_____

3) Why is humility a "necessity" for sobriety? _____
_____
_____
_____
_____
_____
_____

4) List three ways that you can turn from relying on your own will and begin relying upon God: _____
_____
_____
_____
_____

5) Read the following verses aloud in group and discuss what God's Word has to say about pride and humility:

Is. 57:15 *"For this is what the high and lofty One says — He who lives forever, whose name is holy: "I live in a high and holy place, but also with him who is contrite and lowly in spirit, to revive the spirit of the lowly and to revive the heart of the contrite."*

James 4:6 *"But He gives us more grace. That is why Scripture says: "God opposes the proud but gives grace to the humble."*

James 4:10 *"Humble yourselves before the Lord, and He will lift you up."*

1Pet. 5:6 *"Humble yourselves, therefore, under God's mighty hand, that He may lift you up in due time."*

6) What issues of pride do you need to work on? For example some people may have pride in their looks, or their job, or how much money they make.

_____
_____
_____
_____
_____

7) How is our humility essential to our recovery? What would recovery be like without humility? _____

_____
_____
_____
_____
_____

8) Consider and discuss the following verse:

2 Pet. 1:4 *"Through these He has given us His very great and precious promises, so that through them you may participate in the divine nature and escape the corruption in the world caused by evil desires."*

_____
_____
_____
_____
_____

9) Consider and discuss these verses:

Matt. 5:48 *"Be perfect, therefore, as your heavenly Father is perfect."*

_____
_____
_____
_____
_____

1Pet. 1:15-16 *"But just as he who called you is holy, so be holy in all you do; For it is written: "Be holy, because I am holy."*

10) How can we, who are so imperfect, be called to be "perfect" and "holy"?

Many have protested that we cannot possibly stay sober. It is too difficult. Yet Jesus, himself, had these words to say to us:

John 14:12 *"I tell you the truth, anyone who has faith in me will do what I have been doing. He will do even greater things than these, because I am going to the Father."*

11) What things had Jesus "been doing"? What are the "greater things than these" that we will do?

12) What shortcoming do you expect will be the most difficult for you to allow God to remove? Why?

13) What do you need to do to prepare yourself to let it go?

Weekly Updates

The Weekly Updates are an important part of the process of developing the new skills that the 12 Steps teach us. Each week, until you have completed this step, make time to check in with each group member on these items:

1. Did you make any new coping cards during the past week? If yes, describe them.
_____
_____
_____
_____
_____
_____

2. Did you use the coping cards during this past week? If yes, were they helpful? If they were not helpful, how can you modify them to make them so? If you did not use them, why not? _____
_____
_____
_____
_____
_____
_____

3. How has your prayer life changed since you started working the steps?
_____
_____
_____
_____
_____
_____

4. Has your experience of God changed during this time? If yes how?
_____
_____
_____
_____
_____

5. Create your own follow up items for the group.

   a. _____
   b. _____

6. For week two and beyond of Step Seven work, follow up on the character defect work (follow up on this work for a minimum of 8 weeks):

a. What defect did you work on allowing God to remove this week? _____
_____
_____
_____
_____

b. What difficulties did you face with your "defectomys"? (defect removal surgery) ____
_____
_____
_____
_____

c. Did you use your accountability partners as planned for this work? _____
_____
_____
_____
_____

d. What successes did you have? _____
_____
_____
_____

e. What changes to your defect removal work will you make for the coming week? ____
_____
_____
_____
_____

Group Activity

For the coming week, select one character defect that you are ready to allow God to remove. Ask two other members of the group to serve as accountability partners for you in your continued work at allowing God to remove your character defects. Take a few minutes to describe to the group what defect you are willing to have God remove.

a) The defect I am going to work to allow God to remove is: _____
_____
_____
_____

b) My two accountability partners are:

(1) _____
    (a) Phone: _____
    (b) Email: _____
(2) _____
    (a) Phone: _____
    (b) Email: _____

Step Eight

Made a list of all persons we had harmed, and became willing to make amends to them all.

> "If we've continually harmed people and haven't made any effort toward amends, then we've got a lot of people, places, and things to avoid. Large areas of life become closed off to us. When we're willing to make amends, those areas open up again. We don't have to avoid people any more. This is true not only for people in recovery but for all of us."
>
> — *Hazelton Research "Alive and Well"*
> *March 5, 2007*

Step Eight is a step of preparation; in this case, for the work we will have to do in Step Nine. It also takes us, once again, through our past behaviors, and presents us with the task of learning how to change our stripes. The spiritual principles we apply in this step are: Responsibility, repentance, and forgiveness.

Responsibility begins when we first admit to ourselves that we have a problem. It continues as we work through these steps and process what harm we have done, and to whom. Responsibility comes into its fullness when we have completed making an amends successfully.

Repentance is the pivot point for a change of direction in our behaviors. It is the moment when we realize that what we have done, or what we have believed, was wrong. We may have *known* that those things were wrong, but continued to do them. When we repent, we have come to *believe* and understand that wrongness, and no longer have the rationalizations and denial that make it OK for us to continue the behavior or belief. Repentance, when paired with its sister concept, commitment, results in a changed lifestyle.

Our spiritual principle, forgiveness, comes as we forgive ourselves for who we have been and what we have done, and as others extend their forgiveness to us as well. In truth, forgiveness is the only path of salvation whether that be spiritually or emotionally.

Many have asked, "Why are amends necessary?" "Isn't it better," they say, "to let sleeping dogs lie?" It is true that in some cases it is better to not offer an amends, and the discussion of the issues surrounding the decision to offer the amends or not will be addressed in Step Nine. In this step, we are working on being "willing" to make the amends. With that said, the question still remains, "Why are amends necessary?" In part, amends are necessary to restore our "rightness" with the world. Where we have taken without giving, for example, we have damaged others, and we have left an imbalance in our relations with them, and with ourselves. An amends gives us an opportunity to restore that balance.

An important aspect of amends is that when we leave business from our past unfinished, it prevents us from being able to truly change. Try as we may to ignore it, or pretend it does not matter to us, it leaves a hollow space in our souls that must be restored if we are to have any lasting peace. Some have said that having to make an amends is the truest definition of justice.

> *"Then justice shall dwell in the wilderness;*
> *and righteousness shall abide in the fruitful field."*
>
> — *Isaiah 32:16 (KJV)*

Group Discussion Questions

Group discussions about this step will be most productive if everyone has completed the individual step work from the *WTFH? Study Guide for Individuals*.

1) What is an amends? _____
_____
_____
_____
_____
_____

2) Why does making an amends mean that I have to do more than say, "I'm sorry"?
_____
_____
_____
_____
_____
_____

3) How is making amends a commitment to a continuous process of change?
_____
_____
_____
_____
_____
_____

4) Have I made a COMPLETE list of persons I have harmed? If not, who did I skip and why? _____
_____
_____
_____
_____
_____

5) How do I know if I am truly "willing" to make amends to all of them?
_____
_____
_____
_____
_____
_____

6) Am I truly willing to make amends to them all? If not, what do I need to do to become truly willing? _____
_____
_____
_____
_____
_____
_____

7) What fears do I have about making amends? Am I worried that someone will take revenge or reject me? _____
_____
_____
_____
_____
_____
_____

8) How does the Eighth Step require a new level of surrender to the program?
_____
_____
_____
_____
_____
_____
_____

9) What about financial amends? Do I have faith that God will ensure I have what I need even though I am sacrificing to make amends? _____
_____
_____
_____
_____
_____
_____

10) Do I owe any amends that might have serious consequences if I made them? What are they? _____
_____
_____
_____
_____
_____

11) What names on my Eighth Step list are complicated by circumstances like the ones above? Describe the circumstances: _____

_____
_____
_____
_____
_____

12) What do my sponsor and other mentors have to say to me about these complicated situations? What do I need to do? _____

_____
_____
_____
_____
_____

13) Am I spiritually prepared for making any difficult amends and dealing with the results? _____

_____
_____
_____
_____
_____
_____

14) What have I done to prepare myself? _____

_____
_____
_____

15) Do I owe amends to people who have also harmed me?_____

_____
_____
_____
_____
_____
_____

16) Why is it important that I forgive those who have harmed me before I offer my amends to them? _____

_____
_____
_____
_____

17) Have I forgiven them all? Which ones have I not forgiven yet? What do I need to do in order to forgive them?_____
_____
_____
_____
_____

18) Are there amends with which I will have trouble following through? What am I doing to recommit myself to making these amends? _____
_____
_____
_____
_____
_____
_____

Weekly Updates

The Weekly Updates are an important part of the process of developing the new skills that the 12 Steps teach us. Each week, until you have completed this step, make time to check in with each group member on these items:

1. Did you make any new coping cards during the past week? If yes, describe them.
___

2. Did you use the coping cards during this past week? If yes, were they helpful? If they were not helpful, how can you modify them to make them so? If you did not use them, why not? ___

3. How has your prayer life changed since you started working the steps?
___

4. Has your experience of God changed during this time? If yes how?
___

5. (Create your own follow up items for the group)

a. ___

b. _____
_____
c. _____
_____

6. For week 2 and beyond for Step Eight work, follow up on these items about the impact of Step Eight:

a. Have you completed your amends list yet? If yes, how has making the list impacted you? If no, why not? What changes do you need to make this week in order to be able to complete the list? _____
_____
_____

f. Have you become completely willing to make amends to those on your list? If yes, what feelings do you have about making any of these amends? If no, what is in the way for you being able to become willing? What will you do this week to work on that?____
_____
_____

g. Have you reviewed your list with your accountability partners and sponsor? What feedback have they given you? _____
_____

h. Have you spiritually prepared yourself for making the amends? If yes, describe what steps you took. If no, what do you need to do to become spiritually prepared? What will you work on this week towards that goal? _____
_____
_____

Group Activity

Just as we did for our Step Six work on preparing for Step Seven, this week we want to begin our preparations for Step Nine. We will need to create our amends list and make all of the preparations necessary before we actually make any amends (See the appropriate sections of the *WTFH? Guide for Individuals* for details on how to work Steps Eight and Nine). Please note that the group is not ready to move forward to Step Nine until Step Eight has been completed by all members.

This is one of those weeks where it is essential to have prepared your work for this week in advance. Share the top three most difficult amends you will have to make with the group. Discuss one of those in detail each week and ask for feedback from the group. The space below is just sufficient for you to make a couple of reminder notes for yourself, you may need to bring your individual work with you to refer to for details.

My Three Most Difficult Amends To Make Are:

1) _____
_____
_____

2) _____
_____
_____

3) _____
_____
_____

Step Nine

Made direct amends to such people wherever possible, except when to do so would injure them or others.

A few words about amends: Direct, indirect, partial, and written: These are the types of amends with which we will have to work. A few concepts to consider: Amends, apologies, and respect. An apology is not a synonym for amends and respect is the underlying principle to guide all our decisions in Step 9. Finally, a few principles to apply when working Step 9: Respect, patience, and peace. We must practice patience in arranging the timing of an amends with our amendees, we must respect boundaries set by them or others, and peace, for ourselves and our fellow man, is the outcome we pray for as a result of our efforts.

"To amends or not to amends?" that is the question. Step Nine provides the only guidance needed when deciding whether to make an amends or not: When to do so would injure our amendee or others. A harder question to answer is how to *know* if our amends would injure someone. Sometimes the best solution is to ask permission from your amendee to conduct the amends. They are, after all, the final judge on whether receiving your amends would be harmful to themselves or not.

However, before we approach an amendee, we do the best we can to anticipate the impact of our amends. There are many ways in which an amends may harm someone. For example, if the amends will communicate to them information which they did not have at all, or which they may have had only in part, then that information is potentially very harmful. A common situation is where a spouse or significant other does not know any or all of the facts of the addict's behaviors. When the spouse is asking for that information is one situation, and where the spouse is not asking for that information is an entirely different matter. Therefore, we prayerfully seek the wisdom and guidance of sponsors, pastors, counselors, mentors, accountability partners, and others whose opinions we respect. When the potential for harm is reasonable, we leave it in God's hands to resolve, and we practice the spiritual principle of patience. With all other situations, we approach our prospective amendee slowly and carefully, fully respecting any boundaries they may assert.

Sometimes, direct amends are not possible, or advisable. We must be careful not to clear our own conscience at the expense of someone else. In this case, your amends can be an indirect one. For example, if before recovery, we were liars, in recovery we become diligent at maintaining honesty in our relationships. Since an important component of amends is change, in this case, our integrity becomes an excellent indirect amends.

Group Discussion Questions

1) What does it mean to make an amends? _____
_____
_____
_____
_____
_____

2) How do you define the difference between an apology and an amends? _____
_____
_____
_____
_____
_____
_____

3) Is it possible to make an apology without making an amends? _____
_____
_____
_____
_____
_____

4) What does a "direct amends" look like? Give some examples of what you might say in your amends. Ask the group for feedback. If they were the amendee, how would your amend sound to them? _____
_____
_____
_____
_____
_____

5) How many people do you have to make an amends to? Detail how many amends are direct, indirect, and partial. _____
_____
_____
_____
_____
_____

6) Give an example or two of each type of amends you have prepared. Ask for feedback from the group. _____
_____
_____
_____
_____
_____

7) For any amends that are not direct, describe your motives for not choosing a face-to-face amends. _____
_____
_____
_____
_____
_____

8) Are there any persons on your amends list for whom you are concerned that the amends may cause harm to them or others? Discuss each situation with the group and ask for feedback. _____
_____
_____
_____
_____
_____

9) Discuss the various emotions that your Ninth Step work has created in you.
_____
_____
_____
_____
_____

10) How has your relationship with God aided you in your preparations for your Ninth Step? _____
_____
_____
_____
_____
_____

Weekly Updates

The Weekly Updates are an important part of the process of developing the new skills that the 12 Steps teach us. Each week, until you have completed this step, make time to check in with each group member on these items:

1. Did you contact your sponsor this week? If yes, how does talking to your sponsor help you? If no, why not? If you do not have a sponsor, find someone today to be your temporary sponsor until you can find a permanent sponsor.

___

2. Did you make any phone calls to accountability partners and/or group members this week? If yes, how was it helpful? If no, what changes do you need to make for the coming week?

___

3. Did you spend any time in prayer this week? If yes, how was it helpful? If no, what changes do you need to make for the coming week?

___

4. Did you go to Church or attend a Bible Study this week? If yes, how was it helpful? If no, what changes do you need to make for the coming week?

___

5. Did you make any new coping cards during the past week? If yes, describe them.

6. Did you use the coping cards during this past week? If yes, were they helpful? If they were not helpful, how can you modify them to make them so? If you did not use them, why not? _____

7. How has your prayer life changed since you started working the steps?

8. Has your experience of God changed during this time? If yes how?

9. (Create your own follow up items for the group)
   a. _____
   b. _____

10. Follow up on the character defect work from Step Seven:

a. What defect did you work on allowing God to remove this week? _____

b. What difficulties did you face with your "defectomys"? (defect-removal surgery)? ___

c. Did you use your accountability partners as planned for this work? If no, why not? ___

d. What successes did you have? ___

e. What changes to your defect removal work will you make for the coming week?: ___

Group Activity

For Step Nine, we will be making amends wherever possible, except where to do so would harm our amendee or others.

Week 1: Identify "doable" amends from your Step Eight amends list. Pick at least one item from that week for this week and share with the group the amends you plan to make. When necessary and/or possible, schedule the time for the amends and ask the group to pray for you during that time.

Week 2 and beyond: Follow up with the group on any amends you accomplished during the past week. How did it go? How did doing the amends impact you? How is working the Ninth Step impacting your spirituality? How is this work impacting your sobriety?

Note, the group is not ready to proceed to Step Ten until everyone has finished as much of Step Nine as can reasonably be done.

Step Ten

Continued to take personal inventory and when we were wrong promptly admitted it.

"All a man's ways seem right to him, but the Lord weighs the heart."

— Proverbs 21:2

Thus far in our step work, we have worked on cleaning up the mess we had made of ourselves and our world. Our work has also been about how to get and stay sober. Steps 10, 11, and 12 are the maintenance steps, that teach us how to keep the sobriety we have worked so hard to attain. Those who have walked the path of recovery before us teach us to "keep short accounts," and to take a personal inventory on a daily basis.

This disease is often described as "cunning and baffling" because it often seems to us that after we act out we are mystified as to how it happened. "I can't believe I did that again!" we have often exclaimed to ourselves. Step 10 helps us to keep a close watch on our stinkin' thinkin' so that we do not slip and slide down the slippery slope so easily.

Step 10 also teaches us the importance of living each day at a time, each moment at a time. Each moment brings a fullness of life and if we do not drink every drop of it, we will lose a few ounces of something very important, ourselves. By not embracing every moment, we begin to build resentments, disappointments, and frustrations. Therefore, every day we tally our thoughts, feelings and behaviors. We take stock of things we did and didn't do, things we said and didn't say, and things we felt or should have felt.

"In a dark room there is no object to awaken the sense of sight, and you may exert yourself, and strain your eyes, and try to see, but you will see nothing...When the mind's attention is taken up with looking inward, and attempting to examine the nature of the present emotion, that emotion at once ceases to exist, because the attention is no longer fixed on the object that causes the emotion."

— by Charles G. Finney
'Bound To Know Your True Character'

Taking a personal inventory is both a simple and a complicated task. It is simple in that all is required is to conduct a self-check on a regular basis (daily or more often initially) to monitor the presence or absence of certain behaviors, thoughts, emotions, and activities. It is complicated in that, especially in the early days, there is a LOT to track! However, we remember that our recovery and spiritual growth is a process, not perfection. Some of us refer to the Tenth Step as a "mirror check": Every day, we check in the mirror to see how much we look like our Savior, Jesus Christ.

Group Discussion Questions

1) Why is a Tenth Step necessary? _____

2) What does "continued to take" mean to you? _____

3) What areas of personal inventory do you think you should focus on? _____

4) What do you do to take your personal inventory? _____

5) How often do you take your personal inventory? Why? _____

6) Can you skip over small stuff and not promptly admit those wrongs? _____

7) What happens if you do? _____

8) To whom do you admit your wrongs? _____

9) Does admitting your wrongs include making amends? _____

10) Why is the habit of self-discipline so necessary in this step? _____

11) How does practicing self-discipline impact your recovery? _____

Group Activity

The object of this activity is to facilitate your follow-through with applying Step Ten in your life. We all need a little help with creating and maintaining change in our lives, and the group itself can be an excellent tool towards that end.

1. Ask a volunteer to serve as secretary to record the process and decisions of the group.

2. Have the group discuss and develop a format for the daily inventory. We have provided a suggested format in the *Where To From Here? Guide for Individulals* The group may prefer an alternative format, or to use the suggested format as a starting point to develop their own. Spend no more than 15 minutes on this "committee work."

3. Once the format has been adopted, ask the group to commit to using the inventory on a daily basis for the next week. At the next meeting, the group will follow up on the impact of the Step 10 work in Group Activity #2.

Group Activity: Weekly Updates

The Weekly Updates are an important part of the process of developing the new skills that the 12 Steps teach us. Each week, until you have completed this step, make time to check in with each group member on these items:

1. Did you use the coping cards during this past week? If yes, were they helpful? If they were not helpful, how can you modify them to make them so? If you did not use them, why not? _____

_____
_____
_____
_____
_____
_____

2. Follow up on the character defect work from Step Seven:

a. What defect did you work on allowing God to remove this week? _____

_____
_____
_____
_____
_____

b. What difficulties did you face with your "defectomys"? (defect-removal surgery)

_____
_____
_____
_____
_____
_____

c. Did you use your accountability partners as planned for this work? _____

_____
_____
_____
_____
_____

d. What successes did you have? _____

_____
_____
_____
_____
_____

e. What changes to your defect removal work will you make for the coming week? _____

_____
_____
_____
_____

3. Follow up on the impact of your Step Ten Work:

a. Describe the overall impact of the daily inventory on you. _____

_____
_____
_____
_____
_____

b. Do you find that your Step Seven work is overlapping with your Step Ten work? If yes, describe. _____

_____
_____
_____
_____
_____

c. Did you find things about yourself that you need to work on? Describe. _____

_____
_____
_____
_____
_____

d. Did it help you change any old patterns or behaviors? Describe. _____

_____
_____
_____
_____

e. Did it improve your relationships with others? If yes, describe. _____

_____
_____
_____
_____

f. How did it impact your relationship with God? _____

_____
_____
_____
_____
_____

g. Did the inventory improve your sobriety in any way? If yes, describe. _____

_____
_____
_____
_____
_____

h. Are there any changes that can be made to your inventory to make it more helpful? Discuss and implement. _____

_____
_____
_____
_____
_____

Assuming the group agrees, repeat this exercise each week until you have completed Step Twelve. Each week the group will devote a few minutes to discussing these questions and recommit to another week of daily inventory. By the time the group has finished Step Twelve, each member should have developed a good habit of a taking a daily inventory.

Step Eleven

Sought through prayer and meditation to improve our relationship with God, praying for knowledge of His will for us, and the power to carry that out.

> "Watch and pray so that you will not fall into temptation.
> The spirit is willing, but the flesh is weak."
>
> — Matthew 26:41

Step 11 is all about our spiritual growth. Christianity is not a religion; it is a relationship. The Catholic Church, the Baptist Church, and other organizations like these are religions. To be a Christian means to have chosen a personal relationship with a personal God. Step 11 instructs us to be diligent at improving that relationship. Like all relationships, our relationship with God requires an investment of our time, attention, and resources.

Charles was about twelve years old when had was presented with the Gospel in a relational way — that Jesus was the Son of God, who came to Earth to get to know us and to die on the cross to pay for our sins, that we might live eternally with Him. The youth leader explained to Charles that he should think of and treat Jesus just like any other friend of his. He should talk to him out loud if he liked, and to not forget to listen to Him as well. One evening at a meeting with the ministry staff, Charles' mother related how her son had changed since he had given his life to Christ. She asked if they could help her with these changes, as some were a little "weird" to her. A little concerned, the staff asked her to describe what was happening. She explained that Charles had started asking her to set a place at the dinner table for Jesus, so they would not forget that He was with them when they ate. He frequently would come home from school, have his snack in the kitchen, and then run upstairs calling out loud, "Come on Jesus, let's go do our homework!" The youth leader responded, "That's not weird, that's beautiful!"

Step 11 instructs us to seek to improve our relationship with God through prayer and meditation. It has been said that prayer is *talking to* God and meditation is *listening to* Him. Improving our relationship with Him is a process we should work at continually, a task that is never completed, and that we are to work at improving every day.

Step 11 also directs us to pray for knowledge of His will for us, and the power to carry it out. Knowing God's will requires us to allow God to transform our thinking into His thinking, and being able to carry out His will requires us to develop the character assets of humility, obedience, and faith. Are you ready to develop (or to continue developing) these character traits? Then turn the page and let's get going!

Group Discussion Questions

1) Summarize what Step Eleven means to you. _____
_____
_____
_____
_____

2) Think about the people in your life who know you best. Write down at least three or four names. How many of those people do you think would describe you as "humble?" How about "obedient?" Or "faithful?" _____
_____
_____
_____
_____
_____

3) If your life does not demonstrate humility, obedience, and faith, what needs to change about you so that God's character will begin shining through? What steps do you need to take? _____
_____
_____
_____
_____

4) What will be the hardest part of the eleventh step for you? _____
_____
_____
_____
_____

5) How will consistently working the eleventh step change your life? _____
_____
_____
_____
_____

6) What do you know about God's will for your life? _____
_____
_____
_____
_____

7) What things do you not yet know about God's plan for you? For example, you may not know your purpose, what job you should have, whether you should marry or whom

you should marry, or perhaps even where you should live. _____

8) What part of His plan, which you know about, do you lack the "power" to carry out? _____

9) What power is it that you lack? _____

10) How will you get the power that you need? _____

11) Discuss the character assets of humility, obedience, and faith. What are they and how do you know if you have them? Which asset will you work on first and how? _____

12) How can you work on improving your relationship with God through prayer and meditation this week? Write down three things you need to change in your daily life to do so, share it with the group, and ask your accountability partners to help you keep current with those changes this week. _____

Finally, brothers, whatever is true, whatever is noble, whatever is right, whatever is pure, whatever is lovely, whatever is admirable — if anything is excellent or praiseworthy — think about such things.

— Phil. 4:8

Group Activity #1

Prayer and meditation are spiritual practices that require time, patience, and dedication. Not many of us are highly skilled in these techniques. In fact, the idea of sitting quietly doing "nothing" seems rather tortuous or frightening to most of us. The following activity is designed to facilitate the development of our prayer and meditation "muscles" without overwhelming anyone. We practice our familiar recovery principles of "Keep it simple" and "Take it slowly" as we learn these new ways of being.

Praying, or talking and listening to God, is an important tool in developing our relationship with Him. After all, what kind of relationship would we have with our friends if we never spoke to or listened to them? Most of us have found that having a regular time to pray to be an important asset to maintaining our relationship over time. An additional and vital tool is a prayer journal. A prayer journal is simply a record of your prayer requests and the answers from God whenever they come. For example, we may pray for a new and better job. When we receive the job, we may utter a reflexive "Thank you, God," but quickly we forget that God had any part in it at all. A prayer journal stands as an ever-growing memorial of the activities of our Lord in the little things and the big moments in our lives.

Webster defines meditation as, "the turning or revolving of a subject in the mind; serious contemplation." It means to think purposively and extensively upon a concept, like God's love for us, or perhaps upon a specific verse, and to consider it from all angles and implications. As a sponge will soak up water that it encounters, our minds will absorb concepts that we dwell upon. Therefore, we should use meditation to saturate our mind with all things Godly. In Philippians 4:8 Paul tells us to think about whatever is noble, right, pure, lovely, excellent, or praiseworthy. The Greek work for "think about" is "logizomai," which means "to consider" or "to contemplate" in an active and continuing fashion. Meditation is one way to consider something in an active and continuing fashion.

Group Activity #2

Have every member commit to a daily quiet time of six minutes. Spend two minutes reading a passage from one of the Gospels, two minutes meditating on the following verse: *"I am God's child"* (John 1:12), and one minute praying. Take one more minute to record your prayers and any answers from God in your prayer journal.

Or, write them here: _____

Weekly Updates

The Weekly Updates are an important part of the process of developing the new skills that the 12 Steps teach us. Each week, until you have completed this step, make time to check in with each group member on these items:

1. Follow up on the character defect work from Step Seven:

a. What defect did you work on allowing God to remove this week? _____
_____
_____
_____
_____
_____

b. What difficulties did you face with your "defectomys"? (defect-removal surgery)
_____
_____
_____
_____

c. Did you use your accountability partners as planned for this work? _____
_____
_____
_____
_____
_____

d. What successes did you have? _____
_____
_____
_____
_____

e. What changes to your defect removal work will you make for the coming week? ____
_____
_____
_____
_____

2. Follow up on the impact of your Step Ten Work:

a. Describe the overall impact of the daily inventory on you. _____

b. Do you find that your Step Seven work is overlapping with your Step Ten work? If yes, describe. _____

c. Describe the things about yourself that you needed to work on? _____

d. Describe how it helped you change any old patterns or behaviors? _____

e. Did it improve your relationships with others? If yes, describe. _____

f. How did it impact your relationship with God? _____

g. Did the inventory improve your sobriety in any way? If yes, describe. _____
_____
_____
_____
_____
_____

h. Are there any changes that can be made to your inventory to make it more helpful? Discuss and implement. _____
_____
_____
_____
_____

Week 2 and beyond of Step Eleven work: Review your continued work from Step 10, and then review the impact of the quiet time from the past week.

1. Was it hard to keep your commitment to the 6 minutes of QT per day? If yes, what made it so difficult? What can you change to make it easier? _____
_____
_____
_____
_____
_____

2. What was the impact on you of reading the Scripture? _____
_____
_____
_____
_____
_____

3. How did meditating on John 1:12 affect you? _____
_____
_____
_____
_____
_____

4. What did you learn about yourself and/or God from praying? _____
_____
_____
_____
_____
_____

5. Was keeping the prayer journal helpful? Some may not have prayed and received an answer to a prayer in the first week. If that did not happen for you, stay with it and see what happens in the coming week. _____

_____
_____
_____
_____
_____

6. Have the group recommit to another week, according to the following terms: 8 minutes of QT daily. 2 minutes reading a passage from one of the Gospels, 3 minutes meditating on the following verse: I am God's workmanship, created to do good works which God prepared in advance for me to do. (Ephesians 2:10), two minutes praying, and one minute updating your prayer journal. _____

_____
_____
_____
_____
_____

Week 3: Review your continued work from Step 10, and then review the impact of the quiet time from the past week.

1. Was it hard to keep your commitment to the 8 minutes of QT per day? Did the eight minutes seem to go fast or slow? _____

_____
_____
_____
_____
_____

2. Would you say that the having had a consistent QT over the past two weeks was helpful? _____

_____
_____
_____
_____

7. How did meditating on Ephesians 2:10 affect you? _____

_____
_____
_____
_____

8. What did you learn about yourself and/or God from the meditation? _____

9. Do you have any answers to prayers this week? If yes, share with the group. _____

10. Have the group recommit to another week, according to the following terms: 10 minutes of QT daily. 3 minutes reading a passage from one of the Gospels, 3 minutes meditating on the following verse: I am God's workmanship, created to do good works which God prepared in advance for me to do. (Ephesians 2:10), 3 minutes praying, and one minute updating your prayer journal. Here is some space for any notes you need to make on this item. _____

Week 4: Review your continued work from Step 10, and then review the impact of the quiet time from the past week. Discuss the overall impact of the having had a daily quiet time for the past three weeks.

1. Do you see any signs of spiritual growth in yourself over the past three weeks? _____

2. How is your growing spirituality facilitating your personal growth? Please describe.

3. Recommit to another week, according to the same terms as last week: 10 minutes of QT daily. 3 minutes reading a passage from one of the Gospels, 3 minutes meditating on the following verse: I am God's workmanship, created to do good works which God

prepared in advance for me to do. (Ephesians 2:10), 3 minutes praying, and one minute updating your prayer journal. Here is some space for any notes you need to make on this item. _____
_____
_____
_____
_____
_____

Step Twelve

Having had a spiritual awakening as the result of these steps, we tried to carry this message to other lust addicts, and to practice these principles in all our affairs.

> *"What do you think? If a man owns a hundred sheep, and one of them wanders away, will he not leave the ninety-nine on the hills and go to look for the one that wandered off?"*
>
> — Matthew 18:12

Step 12 is, in many ways, the easiest of all of the steps. It certainly is the least complicated. Step 12 asks us to do two things: 1) carry the message of hope for recovery through Jesus Christ, and 2) to practice the principles we have learned in these steps in all our affairs. In other ways, Step 12 is one of the most difficult. It requires us to have the courage to reach out to others who struggle as we have struggled and share our hope and experience with them. This prospect causes many of us to face a sudden, dramatic, and unpleasant feeling of inadequacy. Fortunately for us, we can deliver the message to others in many ways, from the relatively indirect acts of service such as setting up chairs or making coffee, to the very direct "twelfth step call" to go and offer a loving confrontation to someone who has placed themselves and/or those who love them in a dangerous or difficult situation. However we choose to work this step, we remember what we have been taught about sobriety: The only way to keep it is to give it away.

In this step we do what we can to share the recovery we have gained with those who are still struggling. When we share with someone we talk about what it was like for us, what happened for us in our journey to find and keep sobriety, and we talk about what sobriety is like for us now. We think about what it was like for us, early in our journey, when others shared their experience, strength, and hope, and we highlight those signficant moments in our journey that helped us take another step down the path.

Above all, we remember that our responsibility is simply to share our experience and our hope with others. Our task is not to fix anyone else. We will not have all the answers, nor will our message be helpful to everyone who hears it. We do not know what we do not know and are not a recovery-wiki. Our story is only one thread in the tapestry that is our program.

This section is not as much about discussion as it is about action. The questions are designed to first help you prepare to put your twelfth step into action, and the remainder are designed to help you process the impact of whatever things you have done to work your twelfth step. So, get ready, and then get going!

Group Discussion Questions

1) What is a "spiritual awakening" to you?

2) What was it like for you the first time you walked into a recovery group?

3) What was your spirituality like at that time?

4) How has your spirituality changed since then?

5) Have you identified your spiritual gifts? If yes, what are they?

6) What does it mean to "carry this message" to other lust addicts?

7) When you think about sharing the message of recovery to others, what goes through your mind? Do you have any thoughts/feelings which make it difficult for you to choose to work the twelfth step, either completely or in a specific way? If yes, describe. _____
_____
_____
_____
_____
_____

8) If you answered "yes" to number 7, talk with your sponsor, accountability partners and/or other mentors. What are the things you need to do to overcome whatever barrier(s) you have? _____
_____
_____
_____
_____
_____

9) Have you "given it away" yet? In what ways? _____
_____
_____
_____
_____
_____

10) How does serving others impact your own sobriety? Why? _____
_____
_____
_____
_____

11) What are the three most important things you have learned about yourself by working the steps? _____
_____
_____
_____
_____
_____

12) What are the three most important things you have learned about staying sober? ___
_____
_____
_____
_____
_____

Weekly Updates

Carrying the message of recovery to others can be done in numerous ways. Have the group brainstorm ways that your group can work Step 12, either together, or as individuals. For example, the group could set up and staff an information table at your church, or at a local recovery conference. "Ambassador Teams" can be formed to meet with pastors from other churches to let them know about the availability and nature of the meeting. "Service Teams" can be formed to provide various service functions for the facility that hosts your meeting. The team can do grounds cleanup, for example. As individuals, you can volunteer to serve as sponsors or accountability partners to other recovering lust addicts. Individuals can also volunteer to arrive early to set up for the meeting or stay late to clean up. Some meetings have a designated "coffee guy/gal" – who makes coffee for the meeting. This is not an exhaustive list, just a starting point.

1) Update the status and progress of any of your work on the previous steps. _____
_____
_____
_____
_____
_____

2) Update the status and progress of your continued work on Step 11. _____
_____
_____
_____
_____
_____

3) Week 1 of Step Twelve work: Have everyone in the group pick one of the activities from your list and commit to that activity for the following week. Share the item you selected with the group. _____
_____
_____
_____
_____
_____

Week 2 and beyond of Step Twelve work:

1) How did your Step 12 work from this week impact you? _____
_____
_____
_____
_____
_____

2) What did you learn about yourself? _____
_____
_____
_____
_____
_____

3) What did you learn about your sobriety? _____
_____
_____
_____
_____
_____

4) What struggles did you have while doing your 12th Step work? _____
_____
_____
_____
_____
_____

5) How did your Step 12 work impact your spirituality? _____
_____
_____
_____
_____
_____

6) What activity will you work on for the coming week? _____
_____
_____
_____
_____
_____

7) At least once before the group closes this round of step work, pick an activity that stretches you or challenges you in some way. For example, if you have anxiety about public speaking, choose to share your testimony for another meeting, or serve on a panel. Share with the group how the activity challenges you and how you will manage the challenge. _____
_____
_____
_____

Finishing Strong

Congratulations! You have completed your first round at working through the 12 steps. We say your "first" round because most of us will work through the steps multiple times during the course of our lives. Step work becomes a way of life for us because it not only keeps us sober, it keeps us growing, spiritually and personally.

For the last meeting of this group, we recommend that you make it a celebratory meeting. Have someone volunteer to bring a cake, or donuts, or muffins and fruit. Spend some time remembering the highs and lows of your journey together through the twelve steps. Share your plans for the future. Finally, spend some time in prayer together, remembering to give thanks to God and praise Him for the good work which He began in each of you, and which He will continue to its completion (Phillipians 1:6). Congratulations!

Here are some suggested questions for the group to consider. Take each question in turn and allow each member a few minutes to talk about their answer to the question.

1. Briefly comment on the two or three major changes you have seen in your life that have occurred as a result of working these steps. _____
_____
_____
_____
_____
_____

2. Briefly comment on how your relationship with God has changed as a result of working these steps. _____
_____
_____
_____
_____
_____

3. Go around the room and have each member comment about one or two positive impacts that other members of the group had on him/her during this process. _____
_____
_____
_____
_____
_____

4. What was the worst single moment for you during the step work? Follow this answer with your answer to the question, "What was the best moment for you during this step work?" _____
_____
_____
_____
_____
_____
_____

5. What will you do to continue to give back to this program after this step study has ended? _____
_____
_____
_____
_____
_____
_____

Bibliography

Here are some books and resources that have been helpful to us in dealing with the issue of is there a God and Who is He? You can find these online or at your local bookseller.

Spiritual Issues

Josh McDowell	Evidence that Demands a Verdict
	More Evidence that Demands a Verdict
	More than a Carpenter
Jonathan Wells	Icons of Evolution: Science or Myth?
J.I. Packer	Knowing God
Beth Moore	Believing God
	When Godly People Do UnGodly Things
Neil T. Anderson	The Bondage Breaker
Tyndale House	The Life Recovery Bible
Hazeldon	Answers in the Heart
	(Daily Devotions for Sex Addiction)

Recovery Issues

Patrick Carnes	Out of the Shadows
Steve Gallagher	Out of the Depths of Sexual Sin
Neil Anderson	Victory Over the Darkness
	Released from Bondage
Meg Wilson	Hope After Betrayal
Mark Laaser	Healing the Wounds of Sexual Addiction
	The Pornography Trap

Internet Resources

www.rsaministries.org   www.allaboutgod.com   www.blueletterbible.com

www.swordandspirit.com   www.crosswalk.com

www.cptryon.org/prayer/special/index.html

www.ingramcontent.com/pod-product-compliance
Lightning Source LLC
Chambersburg PA
CBHW051453290426
44109CB00016B/1735